JAPANESE IS
NOT THAT HARD

How to Learn the Japanese Language
The Fast and Simple Way

2nd Edition

ERIC BODNAR

ISBN: 9781521529072

TABLE OF CONTENTS

PART ONE

The Method

LANGUAGE LEARNING HELL

Are the Japanese kanji (漢字) characters hard to learn? Are they easy to learn? It depends on how you approach them. That approach is determined by how much language learning experience the student has and the effectiveness of their learning routine. With the right approach and methods, kanji can become unbelievably simple to read and write. It could even become your favorite part about learning Japanese.

Those who are new to learning Japanese and foreign language learning might put themselves through hell to learn the 2,200+ general-use kanji characters. I have a friend who used to share pictures of all the hard work he did to learn kanji. He had pages of his notebook filled to the brim with kanji, and each one has been written ten or more times in an effort to memorize them. My friend was very proud of the work he had done, and seeing his pictures always brought a little extra joy to my day. But unfortunately, he stopped after a few weeks or so.

I remember posting similar pictures myself, but it was of sentences that I copied from my textbook to learn Korean, my first foreign language I studied outside of school. I once identified myself with that level of commitment and hard work. But when it comes to learning kanji, Japanese, and other foreign languages, the value of hard work can be misleading.

Language learning is unique in that way. Japanese is a skill built upon learning and memorizing thousands of words, phrases, grammar structures, and kanji. Reading and understanding this information can be quite difficult, and then, native speakers spit all of this out at seemingly a bazillion words a minute. Many decide to take on this challenge enthusiastically with hard work and ultra-high determination, and I did the same a number of years ago in an effort to learn Korean.

After only a month of learning just a few basic phrases and somewhere around 100 words from my textbook, I relocated to South Korea to work as an English teacher by day and study by night. It was my first time being outside of my home country, and I was surrounded by a new language that I was hungry to learn. For the four years I lived there, there was a determination inside of me that burned red-hot.

It took four years before I realized that something was seriously wrong. At that point, I was confident that I was fast approaching fluency based upon my growing conversational ability and frequent reading of native-level materials like news articles and short stories. Underneath it all, however, was deep dissatisfaction. I wasn't happy at all with the life that I had created.

I chose a life of study and learning, but it eventually developed into a painful and agonizing routine for the sake of more and more progress. This routine was the most effective way to learn that I knew at the time. It helped me to remember more words than any other technique I had used in the past four years.

A major component of that routine was these super difficult flashcards that I created. The front side provided a lengthy sentence or two in English, and I gave myself the task to recall it in Korean near verbatim as written on the backside. They got me to think in Korean and actively recall new vocabulary in the context of sentences. They were also immensely stressful. Stress can be a good thing but not so much for the kind that threatens your mental well-being.

When I would guess incorrectly, I would get legitimately angry at myself. I remember thinking, "I would be fluent by now if only I had the same memory abilities like those famous polyglots. How can these people learn four or more languages when I struggle so much with just one?" I figured that if seemingly superhuman people like renowned polyglot Alexander Arguelles can study eight hours a day, so can I."

I would honor my commitment to learning fluent Korean by spending Saturday mornings and afternoons dissecting entire short stories and newspaper articles line by line. Sundays were dedicated to my three hour grammar book sessions at my favorite cafes in the city. If I wasn't making more tortuous flashcards from new sentences, I copied them down in my notebook in full and recited them multiple times painstakingly. At night, I *rewarded* myself by watching Korean talk shows which did little to keep me interested but was *good* for learning conversational Korean.

I was desperate for change. I had created my own personal language learning hell. It took a close friend to help convince me to start a new life in a new country. I decided to move to Japan and start learning Japanese. Before leaving Korea, I had told one of my Korean mentors about my decision, too. He warned me that I would have to start all the way back from zero as if I was about to lose four years of hard work.

It was one of those rare occasions where I ignored all logic and reasoning and listened to my heart and intuition. It felt so peaceful and zen-like to let go of the baggage that I worked so hard to collect and just follow what seemed to be destiny. I felt free starting over on a blank slate and drawn towards new paths to find more exciting and fun ways to learn languages.

If plenty of linguists and polyglots have mastered multiple languages by themselves without schooling, there was still hope I could get it right. As I tried a completely different path based on putting enjoyment first, I realized I was starting to once again enjoy the mystical and spellbinding process of learning a foreign language.

Starting From Zero Again

Like most Japanese students, I was completely overwhelmed by the kanji during my first year. Learning and jumping from multiple kanji learning resources was most definitely helpful in the beginning, but I would eventually realize a truth far more important. If your Japanese learning routine in general is rooted in highly effective language learning techniques and strategies, you can learn how to read and write the kanji with ease.

For seven years, I read up on hundreds of learning methods and experimented on myself with Korean and Japanese. This includes Scriptorium, Shadowing, audio-based lessons, immersion, language exchanges, flashcards, Anki, online courses, language learning software, memory techniques, extensive reading, news articles, and textbooks. I took the few bits and pieces that were effective in each routine, combined them, and tweaked with them day and night until everything clicked at last.

I had found the routine that I was seeking to quickly memorize thousands of vocabulary words, kanji, phrases, and grammar points with very little stress involved. I enjoy it so much that I felt compelled to write this book to share that method with others who might be looking for more fun and effective ways to learn the kanji and Japanese in general. If the study methods mentioned earlier sound painfully similar to what you have been doing to learn Japanese, I assure you that there is a better way.

Fortunately for you, there is no need to undergo eight hour study routines daily and use medieval-like learning methods as I did in the past. A solid 45-90 minutes of intensive reading and learning followed by a habit of freely reading, listening to, and watching Japanese material for pleasure is much easier to maintain in the long-term. With all the vocabulary and complexity of the kanji characters, it's easy to think of learning Japanese as a test of willpower and determination, but that's not true when you use smart language learning methods and make it fun each and every day.

Why People Fail in Learning a Language

Many dedicated language learners like myself burnout after trying so hard to learn, but the term "burnout" does not quite capture this problem in full. The real issue preventing many people from learning a foreign language is their definition of what it means to learn languages. That problematic definition is formed from being required to take unimaginative and uninspired Spanish and French classes in high school and college. That definition is what causes burnout.

In the beginner phase or at any level, it would be a huge mistake to exclude content made by native speakers for native speakers in the target language. Beginners to language learning often omit this content in favor of more learning from traditional materials like textbooks, online courses, and educational podcasts. I have made that mistake not once or twice but continuously for several years with Korean. Even when I did choose to include them, it was always boring things that were *good* sources to learn conversational Korean from. I forced myself again and again to try to like popular talk shows and variety shows.

There were many things I loved to do in the language, but I didn't understand how to effectively learn from these materials. For example, I loved to play video games in Korean. But do you stop playing to look up each new word that you find? When do you actually just play the game? The hardcore learner that I was tried to learn every new word, and that never lasted past 10 minutes. And when I did let myself play the game, it felt like I wasn't learning anything.

My number one goal for four years was to learn fluent Korean above all else, so progress at any cost was the mindset. It was my vision for my future and a part of my identity. Sure, I had eventually reached a certain degree of conversational fluency but at what cost? Progress blinded me to the fact that my internal fun and motivation meter was gradually sinking and eventually hovering just above zero. And then, it hit zero.

It hit zero multiple times while living in South Korea, a country where I was immersed in the language. Several days would pass without me wanting to doing anything with Korean, and I blamed my laziness and lack of discipline. In hindsight, I can now say that there were two much more important factors that led to these difficult times of zero growth and even regression.

The first is that my language learning methods were poor and perhaps even a little masochistic. The second is my idea of having fun with Korean was to watch Korean TV that I disliked deep inside, yet I forced myself to watch for the sake of learning. I used to think that I disliked it because I didn't understand enough. I thought that once I was able to understand most of it I would eventually come to like it. Now, that may or may not be true, but there were materials that I was clearly more interested in. And I neglected them.

I gave up too easily trying to learn from the things I truly cared about. I questioned their usefulness in everyday conversation. Why would I ever need to know "flaming hydra" and "disintegration beam" from Korean video games when I should be learning practical things like "plant a tree" and "brew coffee"? I repeatedly put off fun materials in favor of more practical ones.

But the truth is that you can learn all of that and learn it easily. This book will show you how to balance all of this practical Japanese and fantasy Japanese and retain it effectively. You can learn primarily from what you love and use it to learn kanji and practical vocabulary as you go along. Love is what makes all of this learning possible. Without love, learning is meaningless.

So, What's the Method?

Immerse yourself in any kind of Japanese material that you love without any English subtitles or translations for roughly 20 minutes or so. This can include reading up on topics that you are highly interested in, watching anime and videos online, reading manga, listening to your favorite music, or even playing video games in Japanese. For this brief amount of time, very carefully listen and look for words unknown to you and that are repeated multiple times. Without stopping the reading, video, or audio, quickly jot down the unknown words that are repeated two or more times and continue without looking anything up in the dictionary. Include the page numbers, video times, audio track times, or in-game screenshots for reference later.

After the 20 minutes or so have passed, stop and review your jotted notes, and pick the two words and lines that you are the most curious to learn. This will be easier to do with written materials, and some effort may be required to find video materials with transcriptions and Japanese subtitles. Next, use online dictionaries and grammar resources to quickly break down the lines to learn their meaning. After fully learning these lines, create very specific reading, writing, listening, and speaking practice exercises in a free program called Anki (www.ankisrs.net). These exercises will help you practice both the lines you select and the more practical example sentences you find in online dictionaries and grammar resources.

As you consistently mine a particular topic, genre, or series and regularly do these exercises, you will come to understand more of it very fast. You'll be actively searching for the high frequency words and learning them. These words are the key to slowly understanding what everyone is saying and what the main idea is. The Anki exercises are just as important in not forgetting those key words. This includes being able to recognize them by eye and ear and produce them when writing or speaking.

If you are in the beginning stages of learning Japanese, this technique is highly recommended as you progress through learning the basics of the language. Reading, breaking down, and learning from native-level Japanese materials like TV, novels, and manga will be difficult at first, but early attempts to learn from these materials will immediately connect you to the real language used by Japanese native speakers every day. This connection will be sure to bring you excitement. It will also help build an early habit of freely reading, listening to, and watching native-level Japanese materials without English.

Learning from the real language has the power to spice up your average language learning routine which is often heavily based on traditional language learning materials like textbooks and phrasebooks. Many language learners never make it past the first book and give up when things become too dry and boring, so this method and the other information contained in this book aim to prevent that from happening. A later chapter will cover how to incorporate this method as you learn the basics of Japanese.

When you combine learning from native-level materials, learning from traditional language learning materials, creating and doing smart Anki exercises, and interacting with native speakers in your free time every day, you will have the foundation for an effective learning routine. How to go about combining these activities will be discussed throughout the pages of this book. The method of this book aims to keep you interested and continually learning until you have reached a level that you are personally satisfied with.

Part I will continue with an explanation about the Anki exercises and how to create them from any Japanese material. Part II will cover how to create your own individualized learning program from the foreign material that you love. I hope you enjoy this book and find it useful in your journey to master the kanji and the Japanese language.

SMARTER WAYS TO LEARN

In general, rereading and rewriting new kanji, vocabulary, and phrases in mass is not very efficient in helping you retain that new information. You may also find it tedious and boring. Anki aims to improve your memory of new information by testing your ability to actively recall it through intelligent flashcard exercises.

I don't like to say the method of this book is flashcards because we were all taught to use boring, primitive flashcards in our school days. I speak of the ones where the front side would read "this animal has eyes bigger than its brain" and the back would read "ostrich." They were dry and dull, and they remind us of the useless facts that we were required to memorize for school tests and forgot just a week later.

In this book, we will look at Production, Cloze, Listening, and Shadowing exercises. Two rules govern these exercises. First, choose easy. Second, choose fun.

These rules act as daily reminders to prevent the burnout that causes many language learners to quit temporarily or indefinitely. These four exercise types will help you to fully understand any new kanji, vocabulary, and grammar that you wish to learn and master. They will train you in all five of the language skills: reading, writing, speaking, listening, and thinking.

This chapter is dedicated to describing the purpose of each exercise, and the rationale behind why specifically these exercises were chosen. A set of examples, images, and how to instructions will be provided in the next chapter.

These Production, Cloze, Listening, and Shadowing exercises use all three of the Japanese writing systems: ひらがな(hiragana), カタカナ(katakana), and 漢字(kanji). Romaji (Japanese written in the English alphabet) is not Japanese, and using it to learn even the basics will place a severe handicap upon your reading ability that is extremely difficult to undo. If you haven't already learned hiragana and katakana, you may want to make that one of your first priorities. Fortunately, reading and writing these characters is an easy task for most folks. If you work well with books, pick the one that appeals to you the most. Any shall do.

If you are looking to learn hiragana and katakana without paying a single cent, there is a countless number of great, free materials online to teach these basic characters. I highly encourage you to treat learning these 92 characters like you were learning the 2,200 general use kanji characters. Writing characters over and over and repetitive reading drills will work for the kana (hiragana and katakana) but are highly ineffective ways to learn the kanji. Training yourself to write them from memory with the help of mnemonics and in the context of vocabulary words will help to prepare you to take on the kanji.

Production

Let us begin with the basic flashcard exercise that you are probably already familiar with. You might have made a few of these if you have ever used flashcards or Anki to help you learn a foreign language. Simply, you'll be given a word in English or a picture and have to say the equivalent word in Japanese. That's it.

For many years I held a strong and bitter dislike for these kinds of flashcards, and I imagine many others out there hold similar feelings. They get really boring really fast. They can give us the feeling that we are back in school cramming for our next test. I abandoned these cards after having much more success with Cloze, Listening, and Shadowing exercises, so why would I ever go back to these stupid things? In recent years, however, I realized that they do have a use.

The problem arises when you do nothing but this exercise in Anki. When you have a strong mix and balance of other exercises to go with this simple one, this exercise is perfect. Our ability to speak a new language is greatly enhanced just by being able to recall thousands of vocabulary and phrases with lightning speed and little to no trouble. We need to know how to quickly say things like red, square, professor, power cable, dehydration, open the door, turn the lights off, and throw a ball. That's where Production exercises in the right quantity can help us.

Putting just the English word on the front side of this flashcard saves a lot of time, and you could also put an image representing the word here in an effort to use as little English as possible. The choice is yours. Abstract words like "nonsense" and "discipline" will be much more difficult to find proper images for, so the English word might be the easiest option. If you are looking to use as little English as possible in Anki, Cloze exercises offer an alternative way to test our recall ability for these abstract words.

Stick with just single words and small phrases. If we put English sentences on the front and try to recall them in full in the target language as mentioned last chapter, we can potentially put ourselves through language learning hell. The possibility of all kinds of synonyms and different translations makes it frustrating. It's possible to check whether or not the translations that we come up with are accurate by getting into contact with other native speakers, but it's highly inconvenient to do this every exercise every Anki session.

Let's say we want to learn from a basic sentence like "冷蔵庫のドアを開いたらリンゴが落ちた" which means "when I opened the door of the refrigerator, the apple fell out." Instead of trying to memorize the full sentence, use these basic Production exercises to help you memorize single words like 冷蔵庫(refrigerator), ドア (door), 開く (to open), りんご (apple), and 落ちた (fell). Make exercises for very short phrases like 冷蔵庫のドア (refrigerator door) and リンゴが落ちた (the apple fell).

What if we reverse the order and put Japanese on the front and English on the back? This would change the Production exercise to a reading and translation exercise, which is useful, yet we will get plenty of reading from the Cloze and Shadowing exercises. Additionally, the Listening exercises will give us a more interesting way to test our recognition of these words.

Japanese Pitch Accent

In these Production exercises, we can test not only our ability to recall vocabulary and phrases but to say these words with correct Japanese pitch accent. Pitch accent makes all the difference between unnatural and natural sounding Japanese. Spoken Japanese alternates between low and high pitch sounds, and it is very difficult to detect and mimic without prior knowledge. Spoken English does the same thing, yet we add stress and volume to our sounds. Japanese does not.

I recommend Dogen's Japanese phonetics series on Patreon (https://www.patreon.com/dogen) if you are looking for something straight forward and practical without too much technical jargon. This kind of introduction and any introduction to pitch accent is important in learning the basics of Japanese. It's only briefly mentioned in most Japanese learning materials, so it is often ignored by many Japanese learners. Choosing to skip over it will result in a very unnatural accent that can be hard for native speakers to understand.

If you were able to successfully recall the Japanese word in the Production exercise but are unsure about the correct pitch accent, check your answer with a free tool called Suzuki-kun (http://www.gavo.t.u-tokyo.ac.jp/ojad/eng/phrasing/index). Simply copy, paste, and click analyze to get a graph of a close approximation of the pitch accent. Don't worry about the settings, as the default ones are more than good enough. This tool can even generate an audio file of automated speaker demonstrating the correct pitch accent.

Cloze

On the front side of these cards, we will be presented with a small context (a sentence or a few sentences) that we learned fully beforehand except that one small piece will be missing. The objective is to figure out what is missing based on the surrounding context and write the answer in our notebook. That missing piece can be a single kanji character, a word, or a piece of grammar. If the missing piece contains a kanji, we should also write or say aloud its reading in the context. This simple exercise will require us to think in Japanese while strengthening our reading and writing skills and building our vocabulary up with virtually no stress.

Context makes these challenges interesting and fun. Test writing new kanji in context. Learn new vocabulary and phrases one kanji at a time. Test for even the easy kanji within new vocabulary and expressions. Test for new word forms and verb conjugations. Test for the correct grammar particle which can be so oddly specific and tricky at times. To summarize, if it is new or unfamiliar to you, make a Cloze card.

There is no need to write any single kanji more than once. There is no need to test for large amounts of missing information. There is no need to copy whole sentences down in our notebook. There is no need to memorize these sentences to recite later. Instead, we will see all of the new vocabulary, kanji, and grammar points again and again in the variety of Anki cards that we will make for each context that we choose from our coursebooks and native materials. While we are testing ourselves on something small, we will still need to use the other information to help us determine the missing piece.

Mnemonics

Learning the writing, meaning, readings to each kanji looks impossible at first sight, but creative mnemonics can make this task not just manageable but incredibly fun and easy. Professor James Heisig, author of "Remembering the Kanji", teaches us that our imaginative memory is much stronger than our visual memory. Writing kanji in Cloze exercises can be a fun exercise in recalling highly memorable mnemonic stories rather than visually memorizing otherwise mundane collections of pen strokes. Think of it as an experiment in imagination.

Whenever you first learn a new character, take just a minute to close your eyes and retell yourself its mnemonic story. Then, write the kanji. Don't try to remember what each character looks like. Don't just copy it into your notebook. Let your imagination do the work.

If you write the characters even just once in this fashion as you learn them, you will know the characters at a much deeper and personal level and not have to review them as much. This alone can cut down your kanji review time in half or maybe even into a quarter. You may not see the power of mnemonics until you start the review process and have to recall stories when your visual memory fails you. It might help you even gain a greater love and appreciation for the kanji.

Heisig's book is highly recommended as a supplementary resource. The book will teach you how to write any kanji near perfectly given just its unique keyword in English. Each story is represented by its unique English keyword which provides a mental map of instructions on how to write the kanji. The 2,200+ general use kanji can all be conquered through witty, silly stories that we create in our minds. When you practice taking English keywords and writing the corresponding kanji, reading them becomes effortless. Practicing from English keyword to writing kanji tackles reading and writing the kanji in one fell swoop.

You may feel compelled to spend hours per day working through these supplementary kanji resources, and I can only hope that the previous chapter offered some incentive to consider other options. A later chapter will expand on how to balance learning from these kanji resources and native-level Japanese materials.

One Kanji Max

I would like to tell a short story to better illustrate this next point. Once upon a time, there lived a young, naive man who used to test himself on two or more kanji at a time. He reasoned that if the combined kanji were somewhat known and simple enough, he should be able to recall it with little effort. Then, one day a card came up during his review, and he instantly recognized outer space (宇宙) was missing. With great haste, he picked up his pen only to become hesitant moments later.

He had seen the word hundreds of times on paper and could say it in Japanese aloud, but he could not write it. He knew that it consisted of the kanjis for "outer space" and "mid-air", yet was that the right order? Was it "mid-air" and then "outer space"? Unable to answer his own question, his confidence shriveled, and he suddenly could not recall how to write either kanji! He could instantly recognize it if it were written somewhere, but how could he not write it? It was then his understanding grew three sizes that day!

Test only one kanji at a time. Imagine that we were learning a new word or phrase composed of multiple known kanji, and we created a Cloze card where we needed to write two kanji. If that were the case, we would have far less context to work with. We would have to remember the exact new word or phrase missing in the sentence from all the possible synonyms. This includes what two kanji made up the new piece of language and the correct order of the two characters. Finally, we would have to remember how to write each kanji. That is far too much!

While we should only test ourselves on one kanji, we can choose to include some hiragana and katakana for vocabulary that require it. If the kanji is used in an adjective, we can test for our ability to recall the kanji and also whether it is an -i adjective or -na adjective like in 安い (cheap). If the kanji is used in a verb or adjective, we can test for the kanji and include the hiragana used in its conjugated form like in 新しい (new). Of course, we may make a Cloze card to test ourselves on vocabulary that are written in kana like たんこぶ (a bump / lump).

Listening

The Listening exercises are simply listening more or less, but text-to-speech services completely change how we can practice foreign listening comprehension these days. There exists a way to take words, phrases, and sentences from any source at all and generate free audio recordings of an automated native speaker saying those words. These audio recordings can then be placed inside of Anki to make listening the easiest and most fun language skill to practice. Amazing nor astounding does not even begin to describe this awesome power now available to everybody.

After hearing a two to three second audio file played on the front of these flashcard exercises, it is our task to either think or say aloud the equivalent in our native tongue. We can test our comprehension of single words or sentences in full here. After the file is played, it's either you get it or don't within three seconds. It's a very simple and effective exercise in training our valuable ears to instantly decode meaning of spoken words just like we can in our first language. The Cloze exercises do take a little time and effort to figure out, but the Listening and Production cards help break up the monotony with on the spot lightning round challenges.

On the back side of these flashcard exercises, I recommend putting the English translation and the Japanese transcription of the audio file to check for complete comprehension. Cloze and Shadowing will be only in Japanese, but using English here is perhaps the simplest way to check if we fully understand the meaning behind the words. Freely listening to and reading native-level Japanese material without English will be encouraged throughout this book, yet this will be one of the rare cases where it may be more effective to use our native language.

Unlike the Production cards, however, we can test our comprehension of sentences in full one by one. Undoubtedly, there are going to be some synonyms when translating full sentences from one language to another, but it takes much less effort to translate sentences from the target language to our native language. Try it yourself and see how fast they go by.

Shadowing

This technique is one way to put more Japanese on our tongues. It was developed and popularized by professor Alexander Arguelles, and in it's original form, it requires long dialogues and short stories as well as adequate space to march back and forth in. I would like to include a very shortened form of Shadowing in our program where we just need to read our selected passages along with a native speaker.

Unfortunately, this exercise can only be done with video and audio Japanese sources, so written materials will be left out. There are methods to get native Japanese speakers to record such lines, but they are highly inconvenient and are generally not worth the time and money to acquire them.

I will admit that this last exercise requires a few hoops to jump through to setup inside of Anki, so if it is too complicated for you, you can practice Shadowing without Anki. I am in love with the idea of practicing a little of everything inside Anki, but I understand that you may not be willing to acquire video files and extract audio from them. Also, text-to-speech robots are not accurate enough yet to imitate proper intonation, so I do not recommend Shadowing after them.

Before or after each Shadowing exercise, it's highly recommended to check where the low and high pitches are located using the Suzuki-kun tool. Listen very carefully to the native speakers again and see if you can pick up the high and low pitches. It's very subtle at first but important to natural sounding Japanese.

You may even want to read the lines with the graph before Shadowing.

To set up this exercise, just place the text and audio on the front side and leave the back side blank. When you are ready, play the sound file by pressing the 'R' button on your keyboard and read along with the audio as best as you can. Two or three times will be good enough. If you found the Shadowing difficult, push the card back only a few days so that you can practice it more frequently.

Shadowing is quite the workout at first, and it remains a good method to build our mouth muscles as we encounter more language to mimic. If you are interested in things like reading at native level speeds, pronunciation, clarity of speech, and accent reduction, this is the technique for you. It's also challenging and incredibly fun.

A moderate amount of Cloze, a high amount of Production and Listening, and a low amount of Shadowing has worked well for me in the past, but feel free to experiment with the ratio. The next chapter will explore one possible way to apply these exercises to new Japanese material.

THE LEARNING MACHINE

Anki will allow us to create all of these flashcard exercises, and it also doubles as a Spaced Repetition System (SRS). The SRS aims to test us on information at intervals just before we are likely to forget. This means easy exercises can be pushed back months and months away until the next time we are tested on them. Difficult exercises will be shown more frequently until we master them. If exercises are too difficult, we can change them to make them winnable again.

We have absolute freedom over what we want to focus on and practice, but this freedom comes at a price. We will have to make our own personal decks based on the materials that we use and what we personally need. We must also stick to a schedule of regularly doing these exercises at a certain point in the day but more on this in the final chapter.

We will see the same sentences frequently during our first few Anki sessions, but soon a large variety of hundreds of sentences will take form. Within a few weeks, we will amass a diverse bank of sentences to practice from, and we will rarely see the same context more than once or twice in a session. Seeing this massive range of words and sentences through the four Anki exercises will do many things for us:

1. Allow us to visit a variety of topics in rapid succession.

2. Test our ability to recall words through reading, writing, speaking, and listening.

3. Keep us on our toes with the uncertainty of what is to come next.

4. Enable learning to flow like a fast-paced game.

How to Setup

When you download, install, and open up Anki, click 'Create Deck' and name it whatever you like. We will only need one deck for now, as all four of our flashcards will go into this deck. Click 'Add' at the top, and then 'Basic' at the top of the new window. By default, you should see four card types.

THE ORIGINAL FOUR CARD TYPES IN ANKI

Let's add Production, Listening, and Shadowing cards. Creating card types for each one takes seconds and allows for easy reference and organization if we ever wish to change something in bulk. If you click "Manage", you can delete the unnecessary cards and keep "Cloze". Click "Add" and select "Add:Basic" and rename it to "Production". Repeat this process for "Listening" and "Shadowing."

Next, you will need an add-on called "AwesomeTTS". It's a free Text to Speech service that we can integrate into Anki. This will allow us to do the Listening card types as well as add an extra audio reinforcement to our Production and Cloze cards. With a simple install and Anki reboot, we can simply paste the word or sentence into the 'Front' or 'Back' box, highlight it, and click the speaker icon from the add-on to quickly generate the audio in seconds. In case, AwesomeTTS is ever removed for any reason, the internet provides multiple free Text to Speech services. Let us take this time to be grateful for this technology and how it makes life a little bit easier.

AwesomeTTS: https://ankiweb.net/shared/info/301952613

Remember to switch card types when creating exercises. To switch card types, if we are looking at a new blank card, click "Type" and select the appropriate exercise.

Inserting Images and Audio

Images and audio aren't required, but they are a means to create a stronger link to what we are learning inside Anki to what we are reading and listening to every day. Images and the original audio files can make Anki all the more real, and your efforts here will be rewarded.

Images and audio from videos can be useful in Cloze and Shadowing cards to add context. They are super easy to insert. Press the 'PrtSc' button (Command + Shift + 3 for Macs) on your keyboard while the video is on the screen and paused at the appropriate moment. Then, we will need to open up a basic image editing program like Paint in Windows (Paintbrush for Macs) and crop the image to our liking before saving it. When adding Cloze and Shadowing cards to Anki, make sure the cursor is in the 'Front' text box, and click the paperclip icon to add our image.

Coursebooks and textbooks provide easy access to native speaker recordings via CD, but inserting audio from native-level materials is a little more difficult.. For educational purposes, you will need to download the original audio, extract video files from the CD or DVD you have purchased, or find the files elsewhere legally. There are of course many ways to create the audio clip we want, but I found the free audio editing program Audacity (http://www.audacityteam.org) to work well enough.

In order to import video files into Audacity, however, we will need to install the FFmpeg library file. This add-on is supported by the Audacity developers and is provided on their website. It can also be found with a simple internet search with the words "FFmpeg library audacity."

<u>FFmpeg Library for Audacity:</u>

http://manual.audacityteam.org/man/faq_installation_and_plug_ins.html#How_do_I_download_and_install_the_FFmpeg_Import.2FExport_Library.3F

After opening the file with Audacity, we can use the times in the original audio or video file to find our selected passage with ease. Use the mouse to highlight the clip needed, press the stop button, and go to 'File' and then 'Export Selected Audio…' to create the audio clip needed. We can use the paperclip icon in Anki to insert these audio clips in Cloze and Shadowing exercises just as we did with the images.

Here's an example of extracting audio from anime:

EXTRACTING AUDIO FROM VIDEO WITH AUDACITY

The images help to add more context. The original audio can make Anki sessions much more meaningful and memorable:

A SHADOWING EXERCISE COMPLETE WITH AN IMAGE AND AUDIO

Example Context

Here's just one way you could make Anki exercises for this sentence:

Sample Context:

彼女は特別な作り方でパンを焼いている。

She has a special way of making (baking) bread.

special

PRODUCTION # 1: 特別

(the act of) making

PRODUCTION # 2: 作り

way (of doing something)

PRODUCTION # 3: 方

(It's) baking

PRODUCTION # 4: 焼いている

彼女は[...]別な作り方でパンを焼いている。

CLOZE # 1: 特

彼女は特[...]な作り方
でパンを焼いている。

CLOZE # 2: 別

彼女は特別な作り方で

パンを[...]いている。

CLOZE # 3: 焼

彼女は特別[...]作り方
でパンを焼いている。

CLOZE # 4: *な*, GRAMMATICAL RULE WITH JAPANESE ADJECTIVES

特別

(Audio file)

LISTENING # 1: SPECIAL

作り

(Audio file)

LISTENING # 2: (THE ACT OF) MAKING

作り方

(Audio file)

LISTENING # 3: WAY OF MAKING

焼いている

(Audio file)

LISTENING # 4: (IT'S) BAKING

彼女は特別な作り方で

パンを焼いている。

(Text + Audio)

SHADOWING # 1

彼女は特別な作り方で

パンを焼いている。。

(Text + Audio)

SHADOWING # 2

One single Shadowing card will be swallowed in a sea of 10 or more Cloze and Listening cards, so one duplicate Shadowing card was created for that reason. Anki does not allow for exact duplicate cards, so we can add a tiny character like a period at the end of the sentence on the front side to allow duplicates.

PART TWO

Learn From What You Love

ONE AND ONLY
ONE TEXTBOOK

Early attempts to learn from native-level materials like Japanese websites and anime is most definitely encouraged for beginners, but without learning the basics of the target language as you progress, your language ability will be very limited. You're likely to have some trouble getting around Japan if you cannot read and write hiragana and katakana. Without knowing the differences between polite speech and casual speech, you could come off as a little arrogant to Japanese people. Speaking without proper Japanese pitch accent can make it very difficult for native speakers to understand you.

This chapter will be a collection of advice and strategies that you may find useful if you are a beginner or are currently working your way through a textbook. There are so many ways to begin learning a foreign language these days, and I don't wish to dictate an exact process of how beginners should get started. That should be your choice. Start wherever you are drawn to the most!

You will have more success the more you focus on the things that truly interest you. A few people will study phonetics first for months and years focusing on sounding as native-like as possible. In the case of James Heisig, he decided to first tackle the problem of remembering the meaning and how to write the 2,200+ Japanese kanji characters before learning anything else.

In the age of technology, quick internet searches, and YouTube, it is possible to learn anything without even a single textbook including a foreign language. For the sake of streamlined learning, I would recommend a coursebook or textbook but a maximum of just one. A high-quality coursebook does provide well-rounded introductions to foreign languages, solid grammar explanations, and a wealth of words, phrases, and sentences to create Anki exercises with.

Coursebooks and other Japanese learning resources provide a safe and sheltered source for learning, yet it is important to escape this language learning bubble as early as possible. Outside of that is where the true language and culture lie. There may be a set of six textbooks to learn Japanese, but you may only need the first one before you are able to learn primarily from material made for native speakers. Smart Anki use and a habit of immersing yourself in native-level materials frequently can make that happen easily.

Working Towards Immersion

There are three intensive learning activities that require a bit of balancing: learning from the coursebook, Anki practice, and learning directly from native-level materials. If you are unsure about how much time you can commit to learning Japanese daily, start with doing just one of these activities for 45-90 minutes each day. Cycle between them every day and try not to get caught up in focusing on just one. They are equally important.

Whenever you're ready, try two of these intensive learning activities each day. If you can manage such a routine consistently, you will be sure to learn at an accelerated rate. Doing all three intensive learning activities every day is not recommended. When strict study time begins to exceed two or even three hours, you'll begin to run into problems similar to those mentioned in the first chapter.

After these one or two intensive learning activities are completed, you can further build upon your routine by adding in extensive activities to do in the target language. In comparison, these are much more relaxed and laid back. Think of them as Japanese hobbies. After the intensive learning sessions, take at least 20-30 minutes each day to freely read, watch, or listen to Japanese material without English or interact with Japanese native speakers. Unlike the method described in the first chapter, here we aren't trying to learn anything at all. Take this time to enjoy Japanese material for the subject matter alone!

For some folks, this one to two hour commitment might be really hard to follow every day. If you are having trouble with this commitment, aim for just 45 minutes every day. Focus on not breaking the habit at all costs. Consistency builds habits.

Doing Japanese three times a week will not cut it. Languages are not just knowledge but also a set of skills our eyes, ears, mouths, hands, and heads must practice daily in order to achieve fluency. If you can only make the time to watch 20 minutes of video content with no subtitles for the day, so be it. You may not learn much for that day, but these small but consistent actions build towards new habits that will enable you to make this major lifestyle change.

If you wish to learn full-time or go full immersion in your home environment, it is highly recommended to cycle between multiple extensive activities each day in time-boxed sessions of 20-45 minutes for each activity. This includes watching anime with no English subtitles, reading in Japanese on topics that you are highly interested in, and communicating with native speakers. You can also take 20-45 minutes at a time to replace more and more of your life with the Japanese language. Some of these steps towards immersion we can immediately get used to, but others may take years in order to overwrite old habits that are strongly rooted in our native language.

Here are some ideas. Delete all songs in English from your music library and replace it with music in Japanese. Change your computer and phone's language. Delete all non-essential English internet bookmarks and replace them with fun Japanese websites.

How To Master Your Textbook

Your textbook should be your loyal and faithful servant and not the other way around. Do not let it become your master. What I mean is that it should not take up the majority of your study and learning time.

Let these books briefly serve you, and then, dismiss them. Seek 5-10 minute explanations for new language and grammar structures. Don't bother with drills and grammatical exercises if they don't interest you. Don't write words out over and over. Don't bore yourself with the comprehension questions in the book. Understand the gist and get out of there! The four super flashcard exercises will make sure that we receive more than enough practice. Use your coursebook time to feed Anki the new information that you wish to practice.

Here are some general rules that may help clear some confusion on what exercises to make as you progress through your book. For new vocabulary words and set phrases, create one Production and one Listening card. For every major grammar point or topic covered, grab 3-5 sentences and make one Listening and Shadowing card. It's not necessary to turn every new sentence into an Anki card, or otherwise, you might fall asleep before you make it to the next chapter!

Cloze cards tend to work better for dialogues and other larger contexts rather than stand alone example sentences. Short example sentences often do not provide enough context to make the answer clear and unambiguous. If there is a specific vocabulary word or kanji that we wish to practice, multiple correct answers can interfere. Stick with larger contexts to test new kanji and vocabulary with Cloze cards.

If you find a good phrase used in a dialogue or monologue that you would like to master, try creating one Production card, one Listening card, one Shadowing card, and multiple Cloze cards to learn it one word at a time. Yes, that is a lot of Cloze cards. Most textbooks will throw a large amount of vocabulary at you, so an extensive amount of Production and Listening cards will help to balance it out. This will keep Anki sessions fast-paced.

Verb conjugation tables can be tackled with Production and Listening exercises. There is no need to make these cards for every possible conjugation and verb. That wouldn't be easy or fun. Start with just three, four, or five verbs for now. Focus only on the most commonly used forms like the polite form (-ます), the negative form (-ない), the past form (-んだ/-た/-った/-かった), and the passive form (-せる). Rather than make one Production and one Listening for every form, split the conjugations between the two exercises to save time. You can always make more as you learn new verbs.

Remember that all of these exercises should go in one deck to maximize variety during sessions and keep you on your toes. You will never know what is coming up next. Cloze cards will make sure we can write the kanji and use the appropriate grammar particle when necessary. Production and Listening cards will provide those quick lightning round challenges to boost our recall speed and listening comprehension. Shadowing cards will work on our pronunciation while challenging us to keep up with the native speaker.

A Most Common Mistake

Here's where beginning language learners make the most common mistake. It's a mistake that often puts an early end to many hopeful newcomers in learning a new language. There is no need to finish your initial coursebook before you try learning directly from fun native-level materials. You don't even need to finish the book or course at all! Learn what you can from it until you get bored.

Boredom is our brain's way of telling us that we are going to burn out if we continue to push ourselves to learn from the same material day after day. Our brains are smart that way. It knows when something is no longer working. Resistance to learning doesn't mean that we are stupid or lazy. It means to stop and do something different.

It's so easy to blame ourselves for getting bored because we might feel that we should learn all this serious material before we get to learn from fun materials. That line of thinking, however, is not true at all. Learning from fun materials is the key to never getting bored and quitting.

Hop around materials as you personally see fit! Jump between your coursebook and your true interests in the Japanese language. Whatever you truly desire to learn from is where you should go next. Listening to and following that desire is what keeps you learning. That's the secret to wanting to learn and improve each and every day.

Try to learn directly from native-level materials as soon as possible. When you personally make the connection between what you are learning from Japanese learning materials to what you see in native-level materials, that will boost your motivation more than almost anything else. That is how you can eventually conquer all the serious Japanese you feel that you should learn.

Reviewing vs Training

As you work through your first textbook, you may find that creating flashcards is much more exciting and easier than actually doing them. Watching pages turn while we advance to more topics is highly alluring, yet there must be a balance between creating and doing the exercises.

I prefer to think of Anki exercises as training rather than review. Review is something a high school or college student commonly endures to get a high grade on a upcoming test. We aren't reviewing. We are learning. If we can't recall the word or recognize it during conversation, we haven't truly learned it yet. In Anki, we are training ourselves to improve our language skill every day by recalling more and more words faster and training ourselves to understand more of the spoken and written language.

Think of these Anki sessions as training. The boxer must train his reflexes and punches to be faster and stronger than his opponent. The bodybuilder must hit his weak points as hard as he can to bring perfect balance to his body. Language learners must hit new words, phrases, and grammar points from all angles to fully develop all five of the language skills. Just knowing how to punch, how to bench press, or how to read a new word is not enough.

ESCAPE THE LANGUAGE LEARNING BUBBLE

There is no point in time where we become ready for material made by native speakers for native speakers. It is certainly not when you complete that set of six Japanese textbooks. This imaginary point in time where we will be magically ready to understand everything doesn't exist. We don't even need to understand half of everything. We just need some simple rules.

You might feel that you haven't mastered the basics after one textbook, and this feeling may definitely reflect some truth. And what about the everyday things in life in Japan: paying bills, renting an apartment, going to the bank, and working at a company? If you would like to live and work in Japan one day, a certain set of vocabulary and phrases is going to be needed. You may even wish to purchase an additional coursebook to make sure that you don't sound like another embarrassing tourist. Go for it.

This book exists to say that you will have a lot more fun and motivation in the long-term when you supplement what you learn from fun things with these language learning materials. Of course, common sense says to do things the other way around. Then again, you have so many hopeful Japanese language students who begin learning and drop out when things becomes too dry and boring.

Some folks including myself have found a series of coursebooks and textbooks to be interesting in the past because the learning process itself can be exciting. The beginning months can be highly stimulating and intriguing as we learn how to express larger and larger ideas. Some of those in the intermediate stages of a language, however, can testify to what eventually follows after the first few textbooks are completed.

You realize that you still struggle to understand most native-level material, so you buy more advanced books covering more grammar, phrases, and idioms. You go harder in your learning routine and aim to study for more than three hours per day. Grammar explanations become long and winded. And there's always more vocabulary to learn. The first few thousand came easy with a little bit of effort, but now suddenly there's 30,000 that you feel that you are expected to know!

"Fun? There's no time for that. I have to learn more", may be the last words of your motivation before it disappears. It's so easy to become trapped and confined within a bubble of language learning materials. Learning may unknowingly become stale, boring, and inefficient for months and years.

An Alternative Course

Let's use these advanced resources as references to look up any new or unfamiliar language structures when we encounter them in native-level materials. Wouldn't it be nice to quickly drop in, understand the gist of the target word or structure, and be done with these resources? Lengthy grammar explanations can easily be forgotten, yet a large context from a story that we truly care about can burn in our memory for years.

You might not even need any advanced textbook. In the age of the internet, quick searches to many questions can provide an accurate answer in just a minute or two. Online dictionaries can provide the basic meaning to an overwhelming majority of words and phrases as well as plenty of example sentences. If more explanation is desired, internet searches for target sentence structures will reveal resources that provide sufficient explanations to most structures.

As we switch our primary learning source from coursebooks to native-level materials, I recommend that you keep adding to the original deck. There will probably be a backlog of hundreds of new cards that you have created but have not been tested on yet. This information is likely to be commonly found in native-level materials, so let's keep building that strong foundation with our original deck.

When there are already 1000+ Anki cards created from coursebook material, it may take a few days to see the content mined from native-level materials show up during Anki practice. It may be tempting to start that new deck but your patience will rewarded. The new content will show up during Anki sessions if you keep your deck order mixed.

For native-level materials, we will use the same four Anki exercises: Production, Cloze, Listening, and Shadowing. In order for these exercises to be smooth and engaging, we must wisely choose our sentences from native-level materials. We will then need to learn the meaning of the new words, sentence structures, and kanji using online dictionaries, internet searches, and image searches.

Without Love, All of
This Learning is Meaningless

Let's switch our primary source for learning to Japanese websites, dramas, manga, anime, music, or whatever got us interested in the language in the first place. Let this material become our new textbook. Learning from Japanese native-level materials that you truly love to read, watch, and listen to for fun will help sustain motivation for the long-term.

Foreign pop culture and TV do not have to be the end goal in learning a language. There is so much more to a language than what you might find on foreign TV. Regardless of the language and culture, low-quality TV programs can numb the mind rather than excite it. For sustaining long-term motivation for years, it's best in the long-run to find a hobby that you truly enjoy and can learn from in the target language. You will know when you find it. You will stop asking yourself the question, "is this all there is?"

Some folks may just wish to meet, befriend, and be proficient in communicating with Japanese people. In this case, Facebook, Twitter, and other social platforms provide instant gold mines of sentences and passages to dissect. You can bring these written words to life using AwesomeTTS and hear surprisingly somewhat natural renditions of them performed by automated speakers.

You may also find new topics to read up on through social media. Make Japanese friends. Press the "Like" button on new pages. Join Japanese groups that pique your interest. Follow famous people that you admire. These actions will immerse your social feed in only your target language.

If what you truly enjoy is found only in reading materials, so be it. Some of the world's most impressive polyglots claim a strong habit of extensive reading is one of the secrets to their amazing abilities. Shadowing and speaking can be practiced elsewhere, and Anki does provide the Text to Speech support to place that written material in our ears at least.

It is common advice to listen to the target language daily or as often as possible for listening comprehension practice, but try asking yourself this question. Would this audio or visual material add enjoyment to your life or not? The answer is easy to figure out. If it takes more than two seconds to answer yes, it's no.

The Immersion Method

Blogs, comics, books, websites, movies, and TV programs all contain these juicy sentences to break down and learn. If you have ever tried to study any of these materials diligently in the past, however, you know how enormous a task it can be. How do we focus long enough to break down an entire online article or even a short story line by line? How do we not become overwhelmed by websites where everything is in Japanese? How can we study a drama or an anime?

How do we keep up the willpower to continue these unsustainable study routines after just two days? The problem gets worse and worse. We burn all initial motivation pushing ourselves to break down and learn massive amounts of language until the day comes when we would rather do anything than another day of routine study.

Let's now revisit the method discussed in the first chapter but this time go into more detail. Immerse yourself in the foreign material that you love without any English assistance for roughly 20 minutes. As you carefully read, watch, and listen, identify the words unknown to you and that are repeated multiple times. Quickly write down the unknown words that are repeated two or more times and continue without looking anything up in the dictionary nor stopping the reading, video, or audio. Include the page numbers, video times, audio track times, and screenshots for reference later.

After the 20 minutes or so have passed, pick just two small passages that you are highly interested in learning. In the case of audio and video materials, you will need transcriptions. For the purposes of this book, one passage can be a single long sentence, a few sentences, or even brief dialogues (two to three lines).

There is no need to translate entire online articles or manga chapters when looking for these sentences and passages. We don't want to burn ourselves out from over-extending our desire to learn too quickly. A few sentences each day along with fun, immersion, and consistency are key.

There is an amazing process that slowly blooms as you read, listen, and mine a single topic for sentences. When you mine passages over and over from a particular subject matter for weeks and months, you will come to know its most commonly used words and phrases. Once you have a strong grasp on the high frequency words, you will be able to piece together more and more of the meaning of new content from that source as you first hear or see it.

When new kanji, words, and phrases come from a much larger story or plot that you are highly interested in, all that new information becomes so much more memorable. Almost every line has character to it, and they can become unforgettable. It's the power of context.

Forget the Rest!

Listen, watch, or read as you normally do in English. Watch videos and read materials once or twice and no more. Don't watch the same video, movie, or TV episode over and over until you break down everything from it for the sake of learning. I am guilty of doing this myself in the past, and to cite personal experience, it will cause agony and madness to slowly creep in. Learning just a few lines of dialogue from each episode or chapter is enough to move on to the next one.

That last line is so vital to making all of this learning fun, so I would like to repeat it. Learning just a few words or lines of dialogue from each episode or chapter is enough to move on to the next one.

But why two passages and not three passages? Each passage does require a significant amount of work. The process of breaking down and learning the sentences, looking up new words and kanji, searching for answers to potential questions we might have, and creating the Anki cards takes a good chunk of time. Two can take from anywhere from 45 minutes to two hours (including the immersion time) depending on how curious you are and the speed you work at. For the sake of consistency, I recommend two, but three is definitely possible. Four raises a lot of doubts in mind.

Japanese People Do Not Talk Too Fast

Using English subtitles to watch Japanese TV shows, movies, dramas, and videos is an English reading activity with some background noise. You will learn nothing outside a few basic words. You might be tempted to use them to help you focus on the story or relax after an intense study session, but if you choose to use them, native speakers will always talk too fast for you.

They will always talk too fast unless you take the time each and every day to practice trying to comprehend what they mean. But how can we comprehend them in the beginner and intermediate stages when they use thousands of words that we do not know yet? Listening comprehension is a skill that is built through practicing with whatever vocabulary that we do know at the time and relying on context for the words that we do not know.

We will understand the foreign language only by consistently trying to understand the foreign language. Anki exercises are amazingly helpful, but we need every chance that we can get to build towards our reading and listening abilities. Some people like to cite that it takes roughly 10,000 hours of practice to achieve a high level of skill in anything, and this number may or may not be completely accurate. The value of consistent practice, however, is something most of us can agree on.

Listening comprehension is arguably the weakest skill of the average language learner, for most instruction of foreign languages is provided through text or explanations in the learner's native tongue. While audio tracks accompanying language courses are certainly helpful, you may quickly find that they do not provide the volume of practice necessary to understand native speakers out in the everyday world.

While subtitles in Japanese are extremely helpful to learning key moments from video materials, it's poison to our listening comprehension ability. Sadly, these subtitles don't come equipped with the native speakers that you encounter in the real world. So, let's turn these subtitles off, too. They are a Japanese reading exercise, which is definitely an improvement over an English one, but we will get plenty of that later in our Anki exercises and while freely reading native-level material.

We don't have a Japanese mommy and daddy to speak to us every day for 8-12 hours for 10+ years. You can pay tutors to do just that, but that becomes expensive to do every day for even one hour a day. Without these adult native speakers constantly around, our ears remain incredibly weak. We have a lot of catching up to do. Listening to native-level materials every day and the Listening exercises in this book's method will help to alleviate this problem.

If you would like to learn Japanese from music, song lyrics would be an exception to this rule. Singing the correct lyrics is already a difficult endeavor in our native language, and mishearing lyrics is just as common as it is funny. Start with the lyrics and make it a game to work your way towards relying less and less on them. If you don't want to sing and would rather just listen, you are missing a huge opportunity to improve your pronunciation, learn language through mimicry, and have quite a lot of fun.

No Subtitles, But How?

If there are irremovable English subtitles in a video, we can block them from view by cutting out and placing a wide but short piece of thick paper in front of our computer screens. We will not need the subtitles and transcripts until we have found our passages for learning, but until then, train your ears to find the words that are both unknown to you and that are repeated frequently. The moments we desire to understand the most can also become one of our passages for the day. Simply jot down the video time for later reference and don't press pause.

Keeping English subtitles out can be fairly difficult for some folks. You will be tested. You will need determination and faith to fight against the habit of doing everything in English. If allowed even for a brief moment, we feed ourselves the idea that we must understand everything to get the most enjoyment from the material. This idea, however, is a lie that we tell ourselves.

Watch and read things where the premise is easily understandable. You may want to start with material you have seen before, so you can get used to everything being in Japanese while still being able to follow the plot. Despite how good it may be for listening practice, it can be maddening watching the same episode or movie five or more times, so I recommend watching and reading how we normally would in our native language. Once or twice is sufficient.

Work towards building and maintaining a habit of freely reading, listening, and watching without stopping. Do not continually stop to look up words and phrases. Do not look up anything at all until the brief immersion period ends. Trying new material and getting lost quickly is frustrating, but when we do possess something that we personally find exciting and can understand the gist, it's enough. When we finally realize that we do not need to understand everything said and can still enjoy our favorite material, we have won!

Choose Easy

At the end of the immersion time, you'll have a list of words, video times, and page numbers to review, but some of these potential passages could be too difficult for your current level. If you select contexts with four or more unknown words altogether, it's still possible to break down all the vocabulary, kanji, and grammar. Yet so many new words, phrases, and grammar points can raise numerous questions to look up and make the learning process slow-paced and painful.

Repeatedly choosing these types of passages can lead to frustrating Cloze and Shadowing exercises. Shadowing becomes a nuisance when there are too many new words and too much unfamiliar language. Our tongues will seemingly freeze up when the difficulty bar is set too high. During a Cloze exercise, we won't be able to figure out the missing word if there are too many unknown words in the context. These kinds of exercises can cause boredom and make Anki very tedious.

Choosing easy can make learning so much more fun and even addictive. Choosing contexts with just one, two, or three new words allows learning to happen seemingly at a faster pace. When the level of the challenge before us is just at the perfect level, we can enter a flow-like state where our learning becomes much more pleasurable and satisfying.

Encountering New Kanji

The order in which we learn the kanji does not matter. Don't worry about the order that you learn the characters because there is no correct order. Learn them as you encounter them in Japanese materials. Use kanji learning resources as references to help you learn these new characters.

For example, if you are learning with "Remembering the Kanji", we can search for any kanji we want to learn at anytime by copying and pasting the kanji into the Kanji Koohii website (www.kanji.koohii.com) to learn the frame it appears in. We can then flip to that frame in the book and learn its mnemonic pieces. If we do not understand the mnemonics used, we can look them up with the index of the book. After taking a minute to connect the keyword to the mnemonic story within our minds, dismiss the book.

Kanji Koohii is a free and fantastic monster of a tool. Often we may be unable to create our own memorable and witty mnemonic stories to help us remember how to write kanji. Kanji Koohii, however, lists several user-submitted stories that are both highly creatively and time-saving. We can use their stories, add to them, and save them to our user profiles. Sometimes other users will provide just the right story which we can use for ourselves.

I still clearly remember being overwhelmed when trying to read and pronounce words written in kanji during my first year, but those reading problems disappeared when I gradually realized a more practical way to learn them. Don't try to learn the readings of the kanji. Focus on learning vocabulary instead. The readings are dependent upon the vocabulary the kanji is used in, so you'll automatically learn new readings when they come up when learning new vocabulary.

Let's look at an example with the kanji 行 meaning "go". It's a very basic kanji, but it's notorious for having so many different readings. If you looked it up in the dictionary, you might get a headache when you see the ten or more potential readings it has. Since the vocabulary determines which kanji reading is used, what good is this information besides scaring students away? Screw those readings! They are arbitrary and useless to memorize.

Start with just the one reading that you encountered in your selected passage and ignore the rest. Let's say the word 行く meaning "to go" came up in one passage. If you have been learning Japanese for more than a week, you probably already know this word, so let's say you want to learn how to read and write this kanji (行). The only reading that you need to know and test yourself on is the one that is used here (い). Keep it easy and fun. Focus on your mnemonic story to help you write it from memory and its one reading here when used in the verb 行く.

Deal with the other readings as you encounter them in future passages. Perhaps a month later you may find 旅行 meaning "travel" in one of your passages. A quick dictionary check will tell you that 行 is pronounced as コウ in this case. As you keep mining sentences over weeks, months, and years, you'll find 行 read as コウ in many other two kanji compound words like 銀行 and 急行. These い and コウ readings are what you will see most of the time, and you will eventually learn the other readings whenever they surface in whatever Japanese material you immerse yourself in.

Context is king when it comes to memorizing kanji and vocabulary. When we learn kanji through the context of new vocabulary and learn new vocabulary through an even larger context like dialogue from a story we truly care about, all this information becomes much more memorable and meaningful.

Double Check Your Work

Hunting and obtaining the subtitles and transcripts for specific audio and video materials can be a challenge. Yet once they are in our hands, learning straight from the material that you love becomes possible. For instance, we can use the free website http://kitsunekko.net to find Japanese subtitles for almost any anime out there. In addition, Viki (https://www.viki.com) offers Japanese subtitles for many Japanese dramas.

This looks like a good line or two to learn for today:

DRAGON BALL SUPER EPISODE 1

After a few minutes of listening and reading, I have found it:

JAPANESE SUBTITLES FOR DRAGON BALL SUPER EPISODE 1

Once we have broken down the new passages and learned the new words and grammatical information, we will have a far better understanding of their meaning. Understanding the exact meaning behind the words can be tricky from time to time. It can be very easy to miss the underlying tone and hidden connotation in Japanese, and this becomes more apparent whenever any language is translated. Perhaps you have seen the results of this on photos of funny T-shirts or inappropriately translated signs in Asia. We wouldn't want the same thing to happen to us when we spoke or wrote something, right?

We should use the English subtitles to double check the meaning that we came up with in our head. Don't use English subtitles and translations when freely watching and reading Japanese material. After our 20 minutes or so has ended and the passages for learning have been selected, it is OK to check the English subtitles to clarify any underlying tone and meaning in the words. It is highly important to make sure that we completely understand what we are trying to learn before we put it into practice. Language textbooks usually provide English translations for this reason.

All this subtitle and translation talk might sound somewhat contradictory, so here's an easier way to think about it. Native-level materials are for long and extensive listening and reading practice. Subtitles and translations are for short and intensive learning.

How to Learn Vocabulary Really Fast

Ultimately, you may use the Anki exercises any way that you wish, but here is one way to dissect new material. New words and phrases get one Production and one Listening card. New words and phrases containing kanji get one Cloze card for each kanji used (both new and already known). New or still unfamiliar grammar structures get one Cloze card. For Shadowing, make two or even three duplicate cards to help balance out the ratio.

After that, here is where we can take it to the next level and learn hundreds of words with relative ease. Use online dictionaries like Jisho (http://jisho.org) to find one or two sample sentences for each of the new words and phrases from the passage. Create Listening cards for these one or two sample sentences. If they contain the new word or phrase plus two or three new words, it will be too difficult. If they contain just one additional new word, however, that is perfect!

Take this additional new word from the sample sentence and create one Production and one Listening card. From this point, you could learn the kanji in these example sentences and create a few Cloze cards here but be careful not to burn out trying to learn too much. You can repeat this cycle by finding new sample sentences for new words!

Continue for however long you like. In the end, you will create a ton of Production and Listening cards, and this makes for very simple and fast Anki sessions considering they are the easiest exercise. They are my personal favorite way to use Anki, but you might be happier with a different ratio of cards.

If we learned the phrase "do in advance" from our chosen passage for instance, we can do some work and attack it from several diverse angles. Here are five sample phrases that we might find in the online dictionary or in our grammar book: "do homework in advance", "do prep work in advance", "be ready in advance", "tell her in advance", and "pay rent in advance".

CONSISTENCY, ROUTINE, AND HABIT

I remember growing up disliking the word 'schedule' and the idea of scheduling things. It seemed like something for uptight and OCD people who do things in an overly controlled manner. I had this impression that if I started scheduling things, I would start to create these over-the-top schedules in which every last minute contained something to do. There would be no time for any fun!

When it comes to taking action towards creating new habits, however, there is a universal truth that we must face. If it does not get scheduled, it does not get done. We must decide on —and then commit to —a routine that we will follow every day, as faithfully as we can. There must be a very specific time during the day when we will do our passage mining, learning, and Anki training. Otherwise, lesser tasks and distractions sneak in, and the age-old excuse of "I couldn't find the time..." starts coming out of our mouths. That classic excuse signals that we never took the next step to set up a specific time and place.

Go ahead and set a specific time of day when you have 45 to 90 minutes to start on the following routine. I recommend the early morning before work or school or right afterward to make it the most important priority while we still have the momentum to get things done.

Sample Starting Schedule:

Monday - Two new passages

Tuesday - Two new passages

Wednesday - Two new passages

Thursday - Anki 10 new cards / 10 due cards

Friday - Anki 10 new cards / 10 due cards

Saturday —Anki 10 new cards / 10 due cards

Sunday —Extensive listening / reading

I encourage you to play around with this starting schedule and make it your own. This is just merely a template for you to start with and improve on. Test your own ideas and see what brings the most learning and enjoyment to your own program.

Some language learners believe in speaking and interacting with native speakers each and every day starting even from day one. That may require a completely different schedule than what I have provided.

Our brains can be sapped after 45-90 minutes of intensive learning and Anki training, but it is important to take at least an additional 20-30 minutes each day to read, listen to, and watch material in Japanese to keep up the immersion habit. We need to train our ears and eyes daily if we desire to hit high levels of proficiency and fluency.

If you are looking to speed up the learning process, try learning two passages and doing the Anki sessions on the same day. Now, this might take you a little over two hours, so maintaining this level of commitment is only recommended for those feeling extra motivated. Make sure to take some sort of break between these two intensive learning activities. You could do three passages or longer Anki sessions, but switching between these two different activities is recommended to maximize your attention span and enjoyment.

If you are looking to learn full-time or even go full immersion in your home environment, it would be wise to keep our daily passage learning and Anki sessions under three hours. There comes a point in time while learning where you might find it much more productive to allocate your time to multiple activities rather than more study. Activities such as interacting with native speakers or freely watching and reading native-level materials with no English can be done as frequently as you like, as they do not require as much focus as intensive learning does.

You may even need to take one or two days off from Anki occasionally and do things in the target language for enjoyment alone. Sing Japanese songs. Play some video games in Japanese. Read up on Japanese topics that interest you. Watch videos, anime, and movies with no subtitles. Binge watching is highly encouraged!

Lang-8, Italki, and HelloTalk

Shadowing helps our speech patterns to sound more native-like while working to reduce our accent, yet we need to practice communicating our own thoughts and make sure other people can comprehend them. While living, working, and learning Korean in South Korea years ago, I felt great finally being able to continually talk in Korean with friends for hours, yet being understood all the time was another issue. Sometimes, we will string together words and grammar that make perfect sense in our head, yet we will be shocked when the listening party tells us that they have no idea what we just said.

Lang-8 (http://lang-8.com) is a free language exchange website where users make posts in the language that they wish to practice. You receive corrections in exchange for correcting other people's posts in your native language. Users can write about anything. We can write about what has been on our minds all day or even specific topics that we are interested in. When we correct other people's posts, corrections for our entries come within hours.

Personally, I found Lang-8 to be the most effective in terms of time and money. It is very convenient to visit the page at any time, write for 10-20 minutes, and leave to go about our day. Later during the same day, we can return to find the corrections and make sure we never forget them. How? Create Anki exercises.

If you are willing to pay a few dollars a session to speak with tutors face to face, Italki (https://www.italki.com) may be the better alternative. You will need to search for a teacher of your liking, schedule for an available time slot, and be logged on the video-calling software Skype (https://www.skype.com) at that time. Good teachers will send you notes of their corrections, so you will still be able to create Anki exercises from what you have learned. Face-to-face conversation and tutoring does have its advantages, so the decision to use Lang-8 or Italki or both will be left to you.

HelloTalk (https://www.hellotalk.com) is a highly popular app that has opened new possibilities of language exchange through texting. Most language learners rate this app very positively, as it possibly the most convenient way to connect directly with native speakers of almost any language that you are interested in learning. It is a great platform to start organic conversations with other users while you make new friends and correct each other as you both progress. Texting certainly takes the pressure off of face to face conversations in meeting new people through new languages, so this may be the choice for you.

Start With 10/10 Sessions

I would like to clarify some terms to make the follow discussion easier to understand. Anki practice sessions entails doing new cards (color coded blue in Anki) and review cards (color coded green in Anki under "Due"). New cards are cards that we have created but not yet seen during practice sessions. Review cards have been viewed at least once before. So, 10/10 refers to doing an Anki session with 10 new cards and 10 review cards.

The last order of business is set the order of the reviews and change the number of cards per session to 10 new cards and 10 review cards. This can easily be done by opening Anki, clicking on the gear to the right of your deck, and selecting 'Options'. Set 'New cards/day' to 10, and then click the 'Reviews' tab and set 'Maximum reviews/day' to 10. The cards are reviewed in the order that they are made by default, so to make sure we see a nice medley of different words, phrases, and sentences, shuffling the cards is recommended and also easy to do. In do so, click the 'New cards' tab, look for 'Order', and select 'Show new cards in random order'. These settings should be good enough to start with.

100 "Maximum reviews/day" is the current default setting in Anki at the time of writing this book, but if we keep this setting and complete the entire review every day, Anki practice sessions alone will quickly start exceeding 90 minutes daily. This does not include the time it takes to learn new material and create cards for them.

Why not be a diligent student and and do all the review cards no matter what it takes? Language learning is not a test. It is a hobby to do in our free time. It should be fun! Exercising, lifting weights, and playing intense sports all have some pain and fatigue involved but also a considerably large amount of endorphins (the 'feel good' chemical) that we can receive in return. Foreign language learning is the same. We must cap pain and fatigue and maximize enjoyment on a daily basis to create a long-term language learning habit.

The starting recommendation is set at 10/10 cards during Anki practice sessions, and a high amount of caution is advised if you would like to increase those numbers. Put on some safety gloves before touching this dangerous electrical current that can easily shock all the motivation out of you. Dividing Anki sessions into small time blocks throughout the day is a wise idea if you are thinking about doing more Anki.

Doing 50+ cards each day can be highly detrimental to our success. More Anki does not mean more learning and progress if it causes your internal fun and motivation meter to plummet and approach zero. During my days in Korea, I was obsessed with disciplining myself to do more than two hours of Anki per day and trying to cram in more and more Anki cards throughout my day. There was a little pleasure but so much pain and misery. I also stopped doing them for weeks at a time. Let's stop training for the Agony Olympics and hellish ultra-marathons of needlessly long Anki sessions. You will do exponentially more Anki cards just by doing it consistently as a habit.

Even when we hit our personal goals, we will not run out of new things to learn and practice. Consistency with Anki is what will keep us learning until that point and even past it while we aim at higher goals. After a certain amount of time (45-60 minutes for me personally), Anki gets boring even with a good mix of exercises. Stop right before you get bored and keep yourself hungry for the next session.

Experiment with your routine. You could do 5/5 cards every day and still have time to create new cards from new material. If you want to incorporate more Anki practice, a large number such as 25/25 could potentially be done if broken into two or more different sessions throughout the day. Most folks work tiring full-time positions like myself, so doing 10/10 sessions might lead to more consistent results.

Start with 5/5 reviews if you have trouble focusing during 10/10 reviews. Train to grow stronger in both Japanese proficiency and your ability to focus deeply. A habit of waking up and going straight to social media is highly detrimental to our ability to deeply focus. Start your day with morning walks and inspirational audiobooks to draw your focus away from everything happening around you so that you can focus on everything happening within you.

If for whatever reason you no longer like a card or sentence that you learned weeks or months ago, it's time to delete that sucker. Don't continue to learn from material that you do not enjoy and that causes you to lose motivation. This has happened to me for not just a handful of cards. I have forgotten entire decks on multiple devices. I am sure that you will undergo a similar process of creation and destruction. Do not be discouraged. In fact, we should embrace it as part of the learning process and the learning-about-learning process.

The End

Thank you so much for taking the time to read my book! If you have renewed hope for foreign language study, at least a little, please take a minute to review the book now on Amazon if you have not already. Tell me what you liked and disliked, and your suggestions might make it into the next edition.

Please be sure to visit my YouTube channel at Fluent Japanese From Anime for more information, explanations, and examples for the method covered in this book.

(www.youtube.com/c/FluentJapaneseFromAnime)

Printed in Great Britain
by Amazon